Dr. Haneesh Khani is a medical doctor by profession, a writer, and a traveler by passion, working as a medical director of a firm in Kuwait. This is his third book; previously, he has authored *My Letters to the Butterfly* (Pegasus Publishers-UK) and *The Order of Truth and Love* (Austin Macauley Publishers-Sharjah, New York, Cambridge, London).

To all the Travelers around the world

Dr. Haneesh Khani

THE TERRITORY OF UNDERSTANDING

A Mission for a New Vision

AUSTIN MACAULEY PUBLISHERS®
LONDON • CAMBRIDGE • NEW YORK • SHARJAH

ISBN – 9789948733126 – (Paperback)
ISBN – 9789948734994 – (E-Book)

Application Number: MC-10-01- 1120872
Age Classification: E

The age group that matches the content of the books has been classified according to the age classification system issued by the UAE Media Council.

Printer Name: iPrint Global Ltd
Printer Address: Witchford, England

First Published 2024
AUSTIN MACAULEY PUBLISHERS FZE
Sharjah Publishing City
P.O Box [519201]
Sharjah, UAE
www.austinmacauley.ae
+971 655 95 202

To the beautiful land and people of Gaza
To all my fellow human beings
To my father, Hassan Kani
To my mother, S. Noor Jahan
To Habish Kani, Hadi Ahmed Khani, and Hamdan Ahmed
Khani
To my friend, Dr. Shanavas P.C.
To the lovely moments, memories, invaluable lessons, and
inspiring pathways discovered in Meherabad,
Ahmednagar, India
To Meher Archive Collective, North Carolina, USA
Thanks to my motherland India for all the beautiful lessons,
experiences, and pathways that came to me through you.
Thank you, Kuwait, for every blessing that has been sent to
me through this lovely land and its people.

WELCOME TO SOME REALITY REVOLUTIONS

Author's Note

Dear friend,

Hope you are fine and well.

I believe that your life is moving through a beautiful pathway.

Phoenix, a mythical creature revered in various cultures, symbolizes renewal, resilience, and transformation. It is said to possess the remarkable ability to rise from its own ashes, representing the cycle of life, death, and rebirth from time to time. Across civilizations, the phoenix remains a potent symbol, reminding us that even in the darkest of times, there is always a potential for renewal and the promise of a new beginning. The image of the phoenix has inspired countless tales and legends, captivating human imagination with its symbol of hope and eternal renewal.

Understanding the phoenix rises from the ashes of curiosity, fueled by flames of inquiry and insight. It soars through the realms of knowledge, casting light on the shadows of uncertainty. Embrace your wings of wisdom as you journey together through some beautiful pathways of understanding yourself and the amazing and lovely ones around you. That's a BEAUTIFUL LIFE. Its essence is LOVE. Its strength is FAITH. Its truth is UNDERSTANDING. It's a precious BEAUTIFUL SPACE deep in our HEARTS and SOULS. Sometimes, it can't be said or expressed or explained. That TERRITORY is infinite. It's DIVINE. It has infinite freedom and infinite possibilities. It's eternal.

That beautiful INFINITE TERRITORY was born as the name of my third book, and it became,

"THE TERRITORY OF UNDERSTANDING."

I hope you LOVE the NAME.

Creating situations is always a part of any writer's journey. Sometimes through thoughts, sometimes through words, sometimes through stories, sometimes through commas, pauses, and inverted commas, sometimes through silences, sometimes through some things, sometimes through nothing, a writer tries to convey his thoughts, lessons, and experiences to others. All these can sometimes contribute positively to the cause of creativity.

In the connection between reader and writer, there exists a sacred bond woven from words and understanding. What I always believe is that (when I'm a reader) through the pages of a book, the writer extends a hand, inviting the reader into realms of imagination, emotion, and insight. In turn, the reader lends an open heart and mind, embracing the writer's words with empathy and curiosity. This delicate exchange transcends mere communication, forging a connection that resonates deeply within the soul. In this space, the reader is important, respected, valued, accepted, cared, loved, and heard. Sharing of the gathered knowledge is very much important for the sustainability of humility and humanity. In the silent dialogue between reader and writer, empathy blooms, perspectives shift, and hearts find solace in the shared understanding of the human experience.

Humans have an innate connection with the signs and symbols that permeate the universe and beyond. From ancient times to the present day, we have sought meaning in the patterns of stars, the shapes of clouds, and the movement of celestial bodies. Whether through astrology, mythology, or spirituality, we interpret these signs as reflections of our own existence, seeking guidance, understanding, and a sense of belonging in the vast cosmos. In recognizing our interconnectedness with the universe, we find solace, inspiration, and a profound sense of wonder that transcends the boundaries of time and space. Ultimately, it serves as a pathway for seekers to explore the mysteries of existence and to deepen their connection with the divine.

Understanding has great significance in life. True understanding is not merely a destination but a continual voyage of the heart, mind, and soul, where empathy serves as our compass, guiding us towards greater compassion, acceptance, faith, and love. Understanding always involves a combination of emotions. As we traverse the terrain of emotions, it illuminates the power of empathy to bridge and foster meaningful connection.

Through these tales of understanding, we might find solace in the shared experiences, lessons, and love that bind us together, transcending boundaries of religions, casts, color, creed, possessions, profession, gender, time, culture, nationality, and circumstances.

Everyone has their own journey to go through. In those journeys, the intricate landscapes of human connection and empathy always help us to encounter many characters gripping with the complexities and easiness of understanding each other, which helps to navigate the balance between vulnerability and strength.

By acknowledging that "everyone has their own journey to go through," we honor the inherent worth and dignity of every individual, embracing the beauty of our shared humanity. It aims to capture the essence of individual growth, resilience, and self-discovery.

We meet many characters in our journey of life. Through the diverse narratives of behavior and actions woven within the hearts of those characters, we understand and witness the unique path each character traverses, shaped by their experiences, choices, and the transformative power of each introspection. Each twist and turn in the road serves as a testament to the indomitable spirit within us to embrace our own paths with faith, courage, love, and curiosity.

The heart of understanding is always based upon two factors: first, to understand our own reality, and next, to understand the genuine ones around us. This understanding happens through a series of trials and signs, and it is actually a beautiful process from the DIVINE LOVE. Everyone has a story. In celebrating the diversity of human stories, we earn the ability to cultivate empathy and understanding for the myriad journeys unfolding around us. As we realize the theme of each journey, we realize a heaven deep within us.

The real journey is to look deep within ourselves and to find ourselves so that we will realize the beauty of the souls and hearts around us.

A wise teacher never tells us what to do. Instead, they give us the knowledge with which we can decide what would be the best for us. Life is also a matter of moments and milestones. Try to focus on small and wise steps. Rushing destroys the beauty of life. Everything will happen at its own time. The universe and beyond are sustained with a beautiful concept. That concept is LOVE. Love is not emotional. Love is not materialistic. Love is not bargaining. Love is not complaining. Love is not a barrier. Love is not about expecting. Love is heartbeats. Love is giving. Love is grace. Love is infinite. Love is eternal. Love is kind. Love is freedom. Love is real understanding. Love is the way back to our "ALMIGHTY." Let's be on that beautiful path back to "HIM, OUR GREATEST LOVE—OUR DEAR GOD."

To get nearer and nearer to God, we have to get further and further away from "I, my, me," and "yours." We have to renounce our own self. It is as simple as that, though found to be almost impossible. It is possible for us to renounce our own limited self by "HIS GRACE."

"TO LOVE GOD" in the most practical way is to love our fellow beings.

If we feel for others in the same way as we feel for our dear ones, we love God.

If, instead of seeing faults in others, we look within ourselves, we are loving God.

If, instead of robbing others to help ourselves, we would rob ourselves to help others, we are loving God.

If we suffer in the sufferings of others and feel happy in the happiness of others, we are loving God.

If, instead of worrying over our own misfortunes, we think of ourselves as more fortunate than many, many others, we are loving God.

If we endure our lot with patience and contentment, accepting it as His Will, we are loving God.

If we understand and feel that the greatest act of devotion and worship to God is not to hurt or harm any of His beings, we are loving God.

To love God as He ought to be loved, we must live for God, knowing that "the goal of life is 'TO LOVE GOD' and find 'HIM' as our own self."

Centuries of continued sacrifice, service, self-purification, suffering, and determined search have to roll on if the aspirant is to be spiritually prepared for the final realization of "GOD."

Absolutely, our connection to the divine is a beautiful and profound aspect of our existence. Whether through various religious traditions or personal spiritual experiences, the sense of belonging to something greater than ourselves brings comfort, guidance, and a deeper understanding of our purpose in life. It's a reminder of the infinite love and mercy that envelops us all, guiding us towards goodness, compassion, and unity.

Every positive thought is a silent prayer that can help us move toward a bright future if we act upon those positive thoughts with faith, patience, gratitude, and love. In life, what we really want will never come easy. Want and need have different meanings. God exactly knows what we need. God always makes a better way to reach our goals. It's a beautiful process. Trust Him. Never give up. A lot more is to come on your path before your last breath. Good things happen at the right moment, and the right moment is when you receive the real answers. Remember, a phoenix never surrenders to failures. Failure will always inspire the winners as stepping stones to the goals of life. That happens spontaneously as we transform into a new us.

When we embrace the unknown in life, we transform into a new us. Transformations are very important in life. They are the gateway to embracing life's mysteries. Traveling helps us to transform a lot. It leads us beyond the confines of certainty, inviting us to explore the unknown with curiosity and wonder. Through transformation and faith, we learn to appreciate the beauty in uncertainty, finding joy in the journey rather than fixing on the destination. In essence, transformation and faith opens our hearts to love the mystery that surrounds us, enriching our lives with depth and meaning.

This is my third book. The first book is *My Letters to the Butterfly*, published by Pegasus Publishers-UK. The second book is *The Order of Truth and Love*, published by Austin Macauley Publishers-Sharjah, New York, Cambridge, and London. As I'm so grateful that both books connect with the people and the universe, eventually, when they select any random pages of the book (it will give answers to the past, a reason for the current situations, or a hint towards the future according to each one's wishes, dreams, experiences, and goals in life), it became a mountain of curiosity for me to learn more about the connections and signs of the universe. It needed a span of combinations of more thoughts, lessons, signs, experiences, and pathways to attain a new approach to this third book, and I hope you will accept it deep from your heart.

Words are really powerful. They leave a lasting impact, so nothing but good should come out of our mouths. The effects will resonate far and wide. Words should be miraculously portrayed so that they heal, inspire, empower, and encourage anyone who receives them. Words are chosen and must bring smiles to many lives. This is what I have always learned from the great and lovely experiences of my blessed life.

The Territory of Understanding is a journey through the intricate landscapes of human connection set against the backdrop of a world teetering on the brink of chaos. As humans navigate the complexities of love, loss, and redemption, they discover that true understanding lies not in the vast expanses of geography but in the depths of the human heart. The book intends to invite readers to explore the terrain of faith, love, gratitude, empathy, forgiveness, and the transformative power of courage, determination, vision, introspection, and compassion.

This book is also the result of my experiences, lessons, thoughts, signs, trials, and silences. It is intended to give a helping hand to fellow human beings whom this book reaches, according to the great script of our "Almighty," to receive answers and inspirations for everyday life, goals, purposes, pathways, and dreams.

The aim of this book is to sow the seed of love for each other in the reader's heart so that, despite all superficial diversity which our life in illusion must experience and endure, the feeling of oneness through love is brought among all nations, creed, sects, religions, and castes of our beautiful planet.

We all have passions in life. Above all the passions, the real passion of our life is to meet God, the greatest LOVE—not for the heavens, not for hell, but just to look at Him, to see that MAJESTIC BEAUTY, to hug Him, to seek Him, to get a kiss from Him, to thank Him, to love Him more and more, to be ONE with HIM, and to feel and realize the MOST GRACIOUS, MOST COMPASSIONATE, and MOST

MERCIFUL HEART. I believe that is the real goal in life. When He asks you how life was, answer Him: you lived it happily.

Let's not separate based on religions, casts, colors, creeds, possessions, professions, gender, community, nationality, or any other manner. Let's unite. Let's be "ONE" so that "THE ONE" who has sent us according to "HIS PURPOSE AND LOVE" will be "THE HAPPIEST." This is a thanksgiving moment to "THE GREAT ONE" and all of "HIS CREATIONS," whom I have met in this short and beautiful journey of my blessed life. Without you, I would not have learned so well. Without the experiences given by you, I would not have been so strong.

I take this opportunity to wish you all a happy reading. If it touches any beautiful heart, if it gives strength to any fellow human, if it helps you achieve your goals, realities, purposes, and dreams, I'm forever grateful. Never give up on life. Be strong alone. Be your best friend. Be more wonderful. Believe in "Miracles" and be a "Miracle."

Here, I'm dedicating my third book, which speaks less, to convey the deeper meanings of the realities of life to each and every one of you. I'm not trying to teach you anything here. I'm just trying to awaken you.

Thanking you all once again.

With LOVE...
Dr. HANEESH KHANI

Introduction

The very essence of these poems is deeply rooted in spirituality. And the true essence of all spirituality begins with the level of presence and connection you bring to your everyday life. As you slowly learn to let go of compulsive projection of the future and attachment of the past, it is in the present where you will meet contentment. And, as you dare to tread a bit longer in this journey of self-discovery, you will be rewarded and pulled closer to a peaceful state of being where you truly belong.

In the insatiable race for advancement and the relentless drive to success, this world has somehow failed to show precedence to spirituality, which is the true mark of inner fulfilment and inner peace. While this unquenchable race has weakened every part of your being and doused the bright fire within you, through every turn of the page in this book, I hope you will allow yourself to be ignited again, rediscovering empathy, love, and a profound connection with others and, most importantly, with yourself.

Dr. Haneesh Khani has a wonderful sensibility in which these poems are a true reflection of his core values and beliefs. Through themes of love, kindness, and courage intertwined in his poems, his work aims to raise consciousness and dissolve all differences led by inherent goodness and compassion that underpin the true essence of human connections.

I have truly been so profoundly touched by his intentions and the message that this book carries. And I am so eager for you to embark on this very special journey. These poems are truly meditative.

Place this book on your nightstand. Find a quiet place and allow yourself to soak in each word, which will carry you towards moments of uplifts and peace. You are truly a miracle, and let this book be that reminder for you.

If you throw a stone into a lake, you will see that the stone will soon disrupt the still water and a circle will form beautifully. In a flash, that circle will multiply into another, then another. And, before long, the ripples caused by one plop will expand until they can be felt everywhere along the mirrored surface of the water. This book aims to echo its power transformation one page turn at a time—expanding your consciousness, lifting you up, and, as a result, transforming your inner awareness, inviting richer, more connected experiences. These ripples of inner harmony are what the book aims to create within you.

Allow me to start your spiritual reading pleasure with this poem:

O, I surrender my life in your hands.
Take me to the farthest sea,
Show me miracles.
Embrace me in your arms,
Embrace me with your godly warmth,
Dipped in pure love, bliss, and contentment.

Friday, 22 March 2024.

Yet again, I find myself filled with gratitude to say a few words in this very special book. Thank you, DR. Han, for giving me this space; I find myself very fortunate.

If you open yourself to the transformative power this book holds, each word will work its magic within you. I wish you a wondrous journey ahead.

Mika Myrie
Cambridge, England

Reviews

Sounds are born out of silence,
And movements out of stillness.
Poetry is the meaning leading to the eternal,
And the poet's soul strives to create a union.

For not everyone can touch the depths,
Getting into the streams of life.
The whirlpool of fate, sometimes as a gift,
Takes us straight to the door of heavens.

Sometimes the poet's hand,
Playing between the lines with silence,
Touches the soundless strings,
Revealing the depth of the hearts.

I sincerely wish you, dear reader, to discover this real treasure
hidden in your heart.
These poems reflect us.

Mikhail Zheltikov
Russia

Reviews

Dr. Han transforms warmth into this lyrical tapestry. Perhaps you are searching for sustenance in your life, or maybe you are getting lost in this modern world.

May this book fill all the emptiness in your heart and accompany you on the journey to becoming who you want to be.

Not every question has an answer in life, but still, lie down, feel the words, and listen to the echo in your soul.

Enjoy the journey—your journey.

Chloe Cheng
Hong Kong

Reviews

Reading these poems at the end of my day was like a breeze of fresh air, like a light, soft hand touching my heart with love.

I ended up with a beautiful smile on my face, which made me tear up. I thought to myself, this is how easily the poet can spread kindness in the world and almost heal someone's heart, even for just a little moment.

The poet explores love within oneself. He pays attention to how the person delves into self-discovery and introspection about what should be our most rewarding life approach.

He clearly chooses to live a beautiful life full of simple but precious little moments. He emphasizes the happiness within ourselves and the happiness that we share with others—that is all we are.

It is an internal journey of self-love.

Deysi Ramirez
Portugal

How to Use
This Book as Guidance

1. Read in One Sitting
If you may, you can read this book in one sitting. It can be completed in about three hours.

2. The Art of Bibliomancy

Bibliomancy has a long spiritual tradition. Whenever you feel lost or confused, I humbly recommend placing this book in your hand, closing your eyes, and taking a deep breath. Then, turn to any random page in the book. As you open your eyes, let that be your message, and let that be your answer.

You can also turn to any random page every day or night, and it may provide answers from your past, reasons for your present moments, or hints toward your future, according to your experiences, lessons, dreams, purposes, wishes, and goals in life.

3. In search of Peace of Mind
For peace of mind, revelations, and epiphanies, go forward or backward from the page you initially open, and you will receive your answers with explanations of many factors to consider for the path ahead in your life. Try it—open it and receive your answers.

Remember
The most amazing secret in life is to move forward and inject utmost gratitude. Never give up on life and dreams.

ALL THE BEST

The Gift Box

To,

May all your dreams come true.

From,

"Bombs and pistols do not make a revolution; the sword of revolution is sharpened on the whetting stone of ideas. The sanctity of law can be maintained only so long as it is an expression of the will of the people."

BHAGAT SINGH

The Art of Waiting

Learn to wait as time is a gentle stream,
In the pathways of life, it's part of the dream.
There's a season for everything and we must bring patience,
As life unfolds its wonders like the soft breath of spring.

In the serenity of the morning or the calm of the night,
Time weaves its miracle in its own silent flight.
It paints the sky with colors and writes stories in the sand,
Teaching us the beauty of holding a gentle hand.

Look for the sunrise and the stars in the night,
For every moment, there's a pure delight.
With patience in our hearts and a calm steady pace,
We'll find joy in waiting, in our life's sweet embrace.

For dreams take their time like a bud to bloom in beauty,
In the garden of patience they dispel all gloom.
So, learn to wait as time has its own grand design,
In its gentle unfolding, we'll find the treasures of our life.

Hope

When the world said, "Give up,"
Hope whispered softly, "Try till you die."
In the darkest hours when all seemed lost,
Hope's gentle voice bore an unwavering cost.

With courage as your compass and faith as your guide,
You'll conquer the storms that reside in life.
In the face of challenges, no matter how high,
Hope whispers to your heart, "Try till you die."

With every step you take and every tear you cry,
Hope is the fire that never shall die.
So embrace its gentle call and let your spirit soar high,
In the face of adversity, forever let's try.

Miracles

In a world that often seems so cold and grim,
Sometimes miracles are good people with kind hearts.
 They shine like beacons in the darkest night,
Spreading warmth and love and their actions ignite.

With compassion as their self, they lend a hand,
 Helping others to rise and helping them to stand.
Their words are a soothing love, their deeds are their work of
art,
In their kindness, they carry many pieces of a heart.

They mend the broken and ease the burden of the weary,
With gestures small and grand, they make the world less
gloomy.
We find a brand-new start in their kind acts,
Indeed, they are the miracles with kind hearts.

Our God

In the quiet depths of a soul's embrace,
Lies a miracle, a sacred space,
Where a soul meets the divine hand in hand,
A miracle of being one with "God" which is so grand.

When we seek the truth within our very core,
And open our hearts to something more and more,
We find a peace, a purpose, and a love so pure,
The great love of oneness that will forever endure.

In every act of kindness and in every prayer,
In moments of joy and in burdens we bear,
There's a connection of a thread that weaves,
The great love of unity that eternally connects us.

To be one with God is the source of all that's true,
He is the great love that whispers, "I am with you."
 In that divine embrace, we find our path,
The belief of oneness where His love holds us so tight to Him.

Forever Be Your Own

Don't let the opinions of others sway your way,
In your heart's own rhythm, let your spirit soar.
For within your being, there's a light that shines so bright,
A truth, an inspiration, and a guiding star's light.

Embrace your uniqueness, your dreams, and your own inner
view,
Let your soul's song guide you, and let your colors shine
through.
Opinions are fleeting, just like the passing of the day,
But your inner truth and strength will never fade away.

Be the artist of your fate in your own blessed life,
Let the brushstrokes of your passion paint the beautiful gate.
To a world where you're free and where your spirit can soar,
Don't let others' opinions close that beautiful open door.

With confidence and grace, let your heart's fire burn,
For the world is your canvas and it's your beautiful turn.
Forever be your own, don't let your essence break free,
In the beauty of being you, find your own blessed decree.

The Journey of Life

Life is like a winding river's flow,
A journey where the wild winds blow.
Each day is a page and a story's birth,
Moments of joy and the lessons learned on Earth.

We all must sow in the garden of time,
The seeds of hope where our dreams might grow.
Through storms and sunshine, we shall try to find,
The strength within us and the ties that bind us.

Like a bird in flight, we fly and dive,
Learning to live and learning to survive.
In this grand symphony, we each play a part,
With the rhythm of life that intertwines in our heart.

So, embrace the great journey of both dark and bright,
For life is a treasure and a gift of pure light.
In its depths and heights, we learn, survive, and grow
Through every twist and turn, our dear souls shall glow.

The Tapestry of Life

The tapestry of life is an ocean so grand,
Woven with threads of love, by a gentle hand.
Each fiber is a story, and every color is a grace,
In this intricate design of life, love finds its beautiful place.

Love's threads intertwine to form the bindings so strong,
In the melody of hearts where it truly belongs.
From the love of a friend to a sweet lover's kiss,
It's in love's many forms that we find pure bliss.

Through joy and through sorrow, through trials and delight,
Love weaves through our moments every day and night.
It's the foundation of life, it's the guiding star above,
A force that connects all of us to the real essence of our
Creator.

In the story of existence, love takes the lead,
It's the answer to questions we might never need.
The real tapestry of life is a love story so sweet,
A testament to our hearts and in its every beat.

Never to Quit

When the weight of the world brings you to your knees,
And when life's challenges whisper, "Give in, if you please,"
Remember these words and keep them close, but never split:
"If you get tired, learn to rest but not to quit."

In the journey of life, there are many hills to climb,
And moments when you feel you've run out of time,
Rest is a gift and a chance to renew your spirit,
To gather your strength and to rise to your merit.

Though the road may be long and the path may be steep,
In the depths of your soul, keep your dreams safe and sound.
With resilience and courage, you'll conquer each pit.
Remember, if you get tired, learn to rest but not to quit.

In the end, you'll look back at the struggles you've known and strove,
And will find greatest strength in the seeds of resilience you've sown,
For it's in the pauses and in the moments of courage,
You learn to endure, to rise, and never to quit.

The Tide of Faith

The tide of faith, like the waves and the vastness of the ocean,
Is a force within us, vast, powerful, and free.
It rises with hope and it makes us strong,
Its current belief is what life is about.

In the face of adversity, it stands mighty and tall,
The tide of faith will never let you fall.
It surges in your heart as an unwavering force,
A lifeline of hope in your steadfast course.

So, trust in the tide of faith and let it carry you on,
Through the challenges you face, until they are gone.
It's an ocean of belief that will never recede,
No matter how near or far we are from our Lord.

The Precious Seed

In the quiet of your heart, every dream resides,
A vision and a goal, where your true self abides.
Remember to hold it close and don't let it slip away,
For there's a lesson in silence; hear what I say.

Like a precious seed, it needs nurturing care,
Away from the noise and in the depths of your heart.
Don't tell people your dream and let it quietly gleam,
For actions speak louder than the grandest dream.

Let it grow more in the soil of your quiet resolve,
With patience and persistence, let your dreams evolve.
Water it with sweat and feed it with bravery,
In the garden of your soul, let your passion fit.

As it flourishes, watch it rise and take a beautiful shape,
Your dream, like a star, in its own course will map.
When the time is right and when you've proved the unseen,
You'll manifest your dream as a tangible, precious seed.

The Little Things

In life's intricate dance where moments are omnipresent,
It's the little things that bring the greatest life.
A hug that comforts and a smile that's so sweet,
A thank you and a compliment, our hearts beat in them.

A hug as a warm embrace, when words can't explain the pain,
It soothes our souls and eases every pain.
A smile is a gesture, so simple and true,
It lights up the world throughout the whole day.

A thank you as a token of gratitude and grace,
In its humble presence, there is a sacred space.
A compliment or a gift that uplifts and inspires,
It kindles our spirits and sets our hearts on fires.

So cherish these treasures and don't let them depart,
For they're the music of life and they're the art.
In the little things, in these simple expressions,
We find profound meanings through the love we attract.

The Most Powerful Speech

In the domain of words, where voices collide,
Sometimes, it's silence that's our greatest guide.
For in the hush that falls at the perfect hour,
Lies a wisdom and strength that holds great power.

In moments of anger, when words may wound,
Silence can heal and can make peace resound.
It's a shield of restraint, a bridge to repair,
A gesture that shows how much we care.

When others seek solace to share their sorrows,
Your silence is a gift and a sign that you're there.
In empathy's stillness, compassion is realized,
And the hurt of the world begins to unwind.

So in life's grand play, where words often preach,
Remember, dear soul, the lessons silence can teach.
For in the moments when stillness is found,
Silence at the right time is your most powerful speech.

The Heights

Don't climb the heights for the world's grand view,
Climb them so that the world can be seen by you.
In the ascent of life, there's a truth untold,
To discover the world, let your heart unfold.

With each step you take, as you rise and ascend,
The horizons expand, and your vision won't be blind.
In valleys and peaks, the world's wonders unfold,
Life speaks its wisdom as you climb the heights.

It's not about acclaim or the praise that you find,
But the beauty of Earth in each step of your heart.
As you scale the mountains and as you reach for the sky,
You'll find the world's wonders nearby, in your beautiful
journey.

So don't seek the summits for the world's grand applause,
Climb them for the world's countless mysteries and love.
With every new vantage, a new truth is revealed,
Don't climb for the world; climb to see the world unfurl.

When a Smile Met a Tear

Sometimes, a smile conceals a world of quiet ache,
In its gentle curve, a heart may softly break.
Behind those joyful eyes, so bright and free,
Lies a story of struggle, known to only a few.

Tears, the liquid diamonds, may fall from eyes so clear,
Yet they carry a joy, a secret, so dear.
In those unspoken sorrows, happiness can be found,
In the depths of our souls, where emotions are profound.

Life's journey is woven with threads of togetherness,
Each one intertwined, today and tomorrow.
A smile may mask the pain that's hard to convey,
But it's in our silent tears, true happiness may stay.

So when you meet a smile or see tears fall like rain,
Remember, life's emotions are a complex terrain.
Be gentle, be kind, for in every soul's dance,
There's a mix of joy and sorrow in every circumstance.

The Matter of the Moments

Each moment in a day is a gem in its own truth,
With its unique beauty and with its special light.
From the dawn's first blush to the evening's soft hue,
Every moment in between holds something new.

The morning's early rays is a fresh start so pristine,
A canvas of possibilities which are yet to be seen.
The midday's bustling journeys with purposes and focus,
The world in motion is fully alive.

As the sun gently sets and the stars take their place,
The quiet of evening is always a gentle embrace.
In the stillness of night, under the moon's soft glow,
Some dreams take flight as the world rests below.

So let's savor each moment as it comes and goes,
 For each holds its miracle, its beauty and its truth.
In the LOVE of life, they're the threads that unite,
Each moment in a day is a gift of exquisite light.

The Legacy of Life

In life's grand theatre, where we each take our part,
It's the actions of kindness that truly set us apart.
The legacy we build is not etched in stone or gold,
It's the love we give and the stories we've told.

A legacy isn't measured in titles or fame,
But in the lives we touch and in their name.
It's the warmth of a hug and the lending of a hand,
It's in the way we help others stand.

With each act of compassion and each word that inspires,
We set the world ablaze with love's endless fires.
The echoes of our deeds will forever resound,
In the hearts we've touched and in the love we've found.

The impact you make and the love that you share,
It's the legacy of a life, beyond compare.
In the footsteps of kindness, we find our true legacy,
For what you do for others' lives on eternally.

A Lone Sunbeam

In the vast expanse of life, in the crowd's endless stream,
Sometimes, you must stand, like a lone sunbeam.
To be brave, to be bold, for what you hold dear,
Even if it means that solitude you must bear.

When the world's storms rage, and voices unite,
Yet your heart whispers softly to do what is right.
In the midst of the chaos and in the midst of the wear outs,
You stand your ground, come what may.

For conviction is the fire that lights up your soul,
And it's in standing alone you find your true role.
Though the path may be tough and the journey quite long,
Your strength is unwavering and your spirit so strong.

Like a beacon of truth in the darkest of night,
Your solitary stand shines with unwavering light.
For in the depths of your courage, in your beliefs so keen,
You become a symbol, a vision, and a dream.

The Territory of Understanding

In life's entangled design, a lesson we must learn,
That understanding often takes a different turn,
To grasp the depths of life's intricate schemes,
Sometimes, it takes experiencing and living our dreams.

In the shadow of empathy, the wisdom we uncover,
It's through our own trials, our hopes, and our heart,
To truly comprehend another's joy or despair,
We must tread that path and breathe that same air.

For the heartache of loss or the joy of success,
Can't be felt through words or in mere express,
It's the taste of life's essence, both bitter and sweet,
That makes our understanding truly complete.

So be patient with others, for they may not yet know,
The feelings and the challenges in which you do grow.
In their own time and way, they'll discern their truth,
And like you, they'll understand when they, in turn, learn.

A Different Flight

Through the miracles of life, where stories are weaved,
Remember, dear soul, you are not deceived.
Don't force yourself into a space that doesn't feel right,
 For your unique light belongs to a different flight.

The world's a diverse canvas, a spectrum so wide,
And within its grand palette, you have your own stride.
In places that don't embrace your essence so true,
It's a sign to move on to find where you'll shine through.

Like a puzzle piece seeking its perfect place,
You'll find your belonging in life's tender embrace.
Don't compromise your spirit, your song, your own song,
For where you truly belong, you eternally belong.

In the sanctuary of self, you'll find your own grace,
In the acceptance of your heart is your unique space.
Don't force yourself to fit where you don't belong,
For your true home awaits, where your heart will be strong.

The Perfection in Trials

In the caverns of life, where struggles reside,
Like a gem in the rough, you must first abide.
For the gem cannot sparkle without friction's embrace,
Nor can a soul grow without trials it must face.

The pressure and heat, they refine the stone's grace,
Crafting a jewel in its own special way.
So, in life too, where challenges abound,
A person's perfection in trials is always beautifully found.

The hardships and battles, they sculpt character's mold,
In the fires of adversity, the true heart's story is told.
Like a gem's hidden beauty, deep and deeper in the stone,
Your inner strength is beautifully shown in trials.

A facet takes shape in each test and tribulation,
A part of your essence, a piece of your truth.
So, embrace the friction, the trials that befall,
Your true self will enthrall in that strong grasp.

The Love of God

In the vastness of the universe, we ponder and we gaze,
Its mysteries and wonders, like a cosmic, starlit maze.
But beyond the reach of galaxies, where no telescope can reach,
There exists a boundless space, the great love of God.

It's a love that transcends, like the eternal starlight,
A love that guides us throughout day and night.
In the cosmic dance, where planets twirl and spin,
God's love is the force that exists deep within.

It's the gravity of kindness and the warmth of care,
A love so profound, beyond compare.
In the silent whispers of the night's soft and lovely breeze,
God's love is the symphony that puts the soul at ease.

When life's challenges seem vast, like a celestial sea,
God's love is the anchor, setting our spirits free.
In the boundless space of His lovely eternal embrace,
We find solace, love, faith, strength, truth, and grace.

So, as we gaze upon the stars, as we wonder and we dream,
Let's not forget the love, the silent cosmic stream.
For in the universe and beyond, in the realms so broad,
There exists a love, the divine love of God.

The Greatest Soul in All

In the miracles of existence, where souls do reside,
There's one that stands apart, as a majestic stride.
It's the greatest soul of all, in the unimaginable play,
A radiant sun that shines through night and day.

With compassion as its heart and love as its guide,
It stands as a beacon, the real unwavering tide.
In the matter of right times, it weaves a beautiful story,
The greatest soul in all, it's light in all its glory.

It's a soul that nurtures, like the earth's embrace,
A sanctuary of peace and a sacred space.
With hands that heal and hearts that mend,
It's the greatest soul, the truest friend of all.

In the pathways of existence, where stars do shine,
The greatest soul in all, it's the heart of the world.
With love as its language and with kindness as its call,
The greatest soul of all, it unites and it enthralls.

So cherish the divine presence of this soul so pure,
With every breath you take, with every prayer you give.
The greatest soul in all, it's a guiding star,
Lighting the path and love from near to afar.

The Road Less Traveled

Certainly;
In life's vast woods, two paths diverged in view,
One well-trodden, the other rare and dear,
The common way, with footsteps loud and clear,
The other is hidden, veiled in mystery here.

I took the path less traveled by my peers,
Where courage led me past my deepest fears.
Beneath the canopy of dreams and shade,
A journey paved with choices I had made.

The road less traveled, full of twists and turns,
With each step, a lesson I'd come to learn.
The obstacles and thorns that sometimes marked the way,
Taught me strength and courage day by day.

Sometimes, the way grew dim, and doubts did creep,
But faith and hope, my promises to keep.
A heart filled with the echoes of each choices made,
The road less traveled gave my soul a voice.

For on this path, I found my truest self,
With dreams, love, and passions placed in my heart.
The road less traveled, where my spirit soared,
A journey worth its weight in precious moments.

Exceeding the Limits

In the vastness of dreams, where boundless skies unfold,
A poem weaves a tale of beautiful roads, in metaphorical gold.
The heart and the soul daring to explore the vast unknown,

It's beating rhythm whispers secrets only it has known.
Each verse, a soaring bird, defying gravity's embrace,
Paints a portrait of a world where limits leave no trace.
Imagination, the gentle breeze that lifts us to the stars,
In the vast expanse of possibility, we're free from life's
constraints.

Within the lines and stanzas, hope's fire brightly burns,
A testament to the human spirit, where every dream returns.
For in the heart's boundless garden, where limits cease to be,
We find the endless story of what's possible to see.

So let the poem unfold, a tribute to the limitless soul,
A reminder that imagination can make our spirits whole.
In the exceeding of these bounds, we find the greatest art,
For it's in the heart's boundless journey, we truly rise high.

The Pinnacle of Existence

In the realm where souls converge, we find,
The pinnacle of existence, in God's design.
A sacred place, where spirits entwine,
A journey within, where divinity aligns.

Upon the mountaintop, we stand so high,
Closer to heaven, beneath the vast sky,
With each step, we reach out to the sky,
The pinnacle of love, where souls do fly.

In the silence of our hearts, we're reborn,
At this peak, where the universe is sworn,
To guide us, through the night and day,
The pinnacle, where God's grace is worn.

As we climb, we shed our worldly weight,
Nurturing the spirit, sealing our fate,
In this place, where time and space abate,
We meet God again, at the celestial gate.

So let us journey to that sacred space,
To the pinnacle of love, where our hearts embrace,
Where we find God's presence and His grace,
And in His light, we'll forever find our place.

Our Own Journey

In the quiet hush of twilight's gentle embrace,
We embark on journeys in our own unique space.
Each of us a traveler on life's winding road,
With secrets to unravel, stories yet untold.

Like stars in the sky, we shine at our own pace,
Each following a path that's uniquely traced,
No need to compare, or rush, or compete,
In our own special pathways, we find our own heartbeat.

For time is a river, it flows and it winds,
In our own special ways, our own destinies we find,
Let's savor each moment, let our spirits unfurl,
Traveling our own distance in this vast, wondrous world.

So, embrace your own journey, don't fear the unknown,
In your own special pathway, your heart will be shown,
With love as your guide, and dreams as your stance,
You'll find your own distance, your own special dance.

A Single Wise Step

When you step into the pathway of life,
Sometimes, the greatest journey, you see,
Is not in miles or oceans wide,
But in a single wise step, with heart as guide.

Each stride is a whisper of destiny's call,
In that single wise step, you give your all,
For in the smallest footprints, so discreet,
Lies the power to make your journey complete.

A step can mend a broken soul,
And make a wounded heart once whole,
It's not the distance, but the courage inside,
That makes a single step a joyous, life-changing ride.

So, take that step, be brave, be bold,
For in the tale of life, beautifully told,
Sometimes, the greatest journey is not so far,
It's a single wise step, like a guiding star.

Our Lasting Claim

In the crucible of life's toughest test,
Difficult situations put us to the best.
They unveil the truth that lies beneath,
Our patience and strength as our inner sheath.

Through hardships, we find our hidden grace,
In the darkest hours, we set the pace.
For it's in adversity, we learn to stand tall,
Our true patience and strength, they enthrall.

In the labyrinth of struggle, we discern,
The depths of our spirit, the fires that burn.
With each challenge faced, we elevate,
Our noble endurance, no one can negate.

Difficult situations, like a crucible's flame,
Reveal our character, our true name.
In the end, we emerge with hearts aflame,
For patience and strength are our lasting claim.

The Sweetest Memories

In the garden of our lives, they bloom like flowers rare,
Special people, unforgettable, in the tender, fragrant air.
Their presence lingers, like a gentle, whispered song,
In the rhythm of our heartbeats, where they truly belong.

Distance may stretch its arms, but memories bridge the way,
With threads of love and laughter, through night and day.
Like footprints in the sand, they leave an indelible trace,
Their essence, ever youthful, in our hearts continues to glow.

With every passing sunrise, and every setting sun,
Their legacy of kindness is woven in our heart.
Special people, never forgotten and forever etched in art,
In the gallery of our souls, they remain as a masterpiece from the heart.

The Tongue

In moments of bitterness, when anger's flame is near,
Don't use your tongue; let it rest, let reason steer.
For words, like arrows, once released, can never be called
back,
And the wounds they leave behind in hearts can leave a lasting
crack.

Bitter thoughts may cloud the mind, like a stormy, darkened
sea,
But pause and let your conscience guide; choose your words
carefully.
For in the silent eloquence of grace, there lies great strength,
And kind words can heal the wounds, no matter their length.

A tongue can be a weapon or a balm to soothe the soul,
So choose your words with wisdom; let empathy be your goal.
In moments of bitterness, remember there's a choice to make,
To build bridges, not walls, with words that heal, not break.

For once the bitter words take flight, their echo can't be
hushed,
But words of kindness and respect leave hearts forever
touched.
So don't use your tongue when thoughts turn bitter; let love
be your guide,
In the harmony of understanding, bitterness can subside.

Never Limit Yourself

In a boundless world of dreams, where possibilities take flight,
Don't limit yourself; let your spirit shine so bright.
The universe is a canvas, with colors yet untried,
Paint your life with aspirations and let your heart be your guide.

Though challenges may test you and doubts may cloud your view,
Remember, within you, there's a power to transform and renew.
With each step you take, you're sculpting your own way,
In this limitless world, where your dreams have room to roll.

The stars above twinkle, as if whispering to your soul,
"Embrace your limitless potential; let your passions take control."
The winds that gently rustle through the leaves of ancient trees,
Carry the secrets of success and the whispers of life's ease.

Infinite is the horizon, where your vision can unfurl,
In every moment, every choice, you shape our own unique world.
Never limit yourself, for your potential knows no end,
Let you be the author of your story, where dreams become certainties.

Meher Baba

In a world of love and light so pure,
Meher Baba's presence secured our hearts.
Silent master with a gaze so deep,
Guiding souls on the path they seek.

With boundless compassion, more than the vast ocean,
He touched our souls and set them free.
In the silence of his love, a Sufi found,
The truth beyond all sight and sound.

He walked among us as a living flame,
A beacon of love in every heart.
His teachings are simple, profound, and clear,
In every heart, his love did appear.

All worries cease in his embrace,
He brought us a message of lasting peace.
A spiritual guide and a friend so dear,
In "His love", there's no fear.

He showed the way through signs and trials,
To find the truth, come what may.
As a living example of the greatest master,
A love so deep, where we all are known.

So let us remember, with hearts sincere,
The greatest Sufi's love is always near.
In his presence, we find our grace,
A heart-touching truth in his loving embrace.

The End of Civilization

In twilight's somber, fading glow,
A tale of woe, we must bestow,
Upon the canvas of mankind's fate,
The end of all, we contemplate.

Once, cities rose to touch the sky,
Now, their ruins lie and no souls nearby,
Forgotten dreams and echoes lost,
In this same world, where hope rose high.

The rivers were once so pure and clear,
Now run with sorrow, painted in blood,
The earth, once lush, now parched and dry,
Civilization's end draws nigh.

But in the ruins, a spark remains,
A whisper of hope that still sustains,
In the hearts of those who dare to dream,
Of a world reborn, a vibrant gleam.

For though the end may seem so near,
Humanity's spirit will persevere forever,
And from the ashes, we shall rise,
A new civilization, under the skies.

The Return of the Christ

In a world where time unfurls its scroll,
A tale of hope, of a long-awaited goal.
The Christ, in glory, shall return one day,
To guide our souls in a radiant array.

From ancient scrolls, a prophecy foretold,
A Savior's return, His love manifold.
In shadows of night, His star shall shine,
A beacon of hope, a love divine.

With open arms, the world shall embrace,
Christ's return, a wondrous grace.
He'll heal the broken, mend the weary heart,
A promise fulfilled, a brand-new start.

Infinite moments in His timeless embrace,
Revealing truths in every face.
The Christ returns in glory and rhyme,
Guiding us through the vastness of time.

As time marches on with unwavering grace,
We await the moment, face to face.
With the Christ, our hearts entwine,
In the tapestry of eternity, so divine.

Mind Over Emotions;
The Triumph

In a world of dreams, where hope does soar,
The path to success, you're destined for more.
With a mind like a fortress, resolute and bold,
Your journey of triumph, a story to be told.

Let your emotions be waves in the sea,
But your mind, an anchor, steadfast and free.
Don't compare your progress to others, my friend,
For each journey's unique, with no set end.

In the quiet of your thoughts, you'll find the key,
To unlock the potential that's meant to be.
In the depth of your soul, there's strength to explore,
To win more and more, forever and ever more.

For success is a journey, a personal flight,
Guided by your heart's unwavering light.
So believe in yourself, let your spirit unfurl,
You can win more and more, in this wonderful world.

Endurance

Endurance is the flame that lights the way,
A path to greatness, come what may.
With steadfast heart and spirit strong,
We journey forth, though the road is long.

In sweat and toil, our dreams we chase,
For hard work paves success's grace.
Through trials and tribulations, we persist,
With every challenge, we coexist.

The climb is steep, the burden immense,
But within, we find our inner defense.
With each step forward, we grow and learn,
In the face of adversity, we discern.

So hold your head high, and dreams in sight,
For in the darkest hour, you'll find your light.
Endurance and hard work, the keys to the door,
That leads to success, forevermore.

A Bond of Love

In hard times, friends' true colors shine,
A bond of love, so pure and fine.
When skies are gray and troubles near,
True friends embrace, hold close, and dear.

Through storms of life, they stand by your side,
In the darkest hours, they are your guide.
With love, they lift your spirit high,
And with unwavering faith, they'll never say goodbye.

Every dream in life is a precious art,
 Sustained by love that warms the heart.
With faith as strong as oak, it grows,
In the face of challenges, it shows.

So cherish true friends when hard times appear,
Their love, faith, and hope, so clear.
In life's lovely journey, they are the thread,
Supporting every dream, until it's fully spread.

Love: The Eternal Word

In the world of words and ink so deep,
The writer's soul forever seeks,
To craft tales of love and endless skies,
For the writer, lover, and beloved never dies.

With every stroke of the pen, they weave,
A kingdom of emotions, in which they believe,
The lover's heart is a treasure to behold,
Their story etched in words of gold.

The beloved God, a muse of endless grace,
Inspires the writer in every place,
Their soul lingers in every line,
A love that transcends the boundaries of time.

So, let this poem be a reminder true,
That the writer, lover, and beloved, in every hue,
Live on in the stories they create,
As the writer, lover, and the beloved never dies.

The Light from the Beyond

It was dark,
Then the light arrived.
They called it 'Noor',
The light from the beyond.

Seize the Day

In life's great tapestry, we often find,
Moments of hesitation that can bind,
Our dreams and hopes in endless delay,
But if you wait for the right moment, it may slip away.

The perfect time, a mirage, it seems,
A distant vision in our wandering dreams,
For time is fleeting, swift it flies,
In the blink of an eye, the moment dies.

Prepare yourself, be ready to go,
With determination, let your passions flow,
Don't wait for others, their approval to applaud,
Your path is yours, as guided by the Divine, our God.

So, remember, in the grand scheme of time,
Waiting forever is a fruitless climb,
Start now, be ready, and don't delay,
For your journey's unfolding, seize the day.

You

Who you were is a memory held in the past,
A chapter of your life was a shadow cast,
Yet, who you are is a vibrant, living soul,
The future's canvas is where your stories unfold.

In yesteryears, you were but a dream,
As life's river flowed as a silent stream,
But who you are now stands strong and free,
A tapestry of moments, a symphony.

Who you were is a foundation, a start,
But who you are is a work of art,
Each day you grow, learn, and change,
Embrace the beauty of your life's range.

The future holds secrets, yet unseen,
Who you will be is a journey unforeseen,
With every step, you shape your fate,
As you walk the path, it's never too late.

So remember, my friend, in this life's decree,
Who you were, who you are, who you'll be,
Three facets of the gem that you are,
A story, a journey, and a shining star.

We'll Make It Real

In the realm of politics and governance, we dream,
Of leaders who unite, in fairness and esteem,
A vision where they work to save the day,
For the country and its people, come what may.

Let's wish for leaders with hearts so true,
Who strive to build a brighter world for us,
Let's hope for policies that mend, not break,
A future where progress and compassion make.

Let's do our part, in the season of change,
With voices united, we can rearrange,
A nation where the bonds between us thrive,
For the common good, together we'll strive.

Let's relax, in faith that good will prevail,
As we chart our course, let love and peace set sail,
In unity, we'll find the strength to stand,
With open hearts, together we'll expand.

With hope, with love, with dreams in line,
In this vision, everything will be fine,
For politics and governance, a force to heal,
With unity and purpose, we'll make it real.

The Abode of God

In the depths of your soul, don't roam afar,
For within you, God is where you are,
His presence dwells, a radiant art,
In the sanctuary of your cleansed heart.

Let not your search lead to distant lands,
For the Creator's touch is in your hands,
With every beat, a sacred part,
God resides within as a work of divine art.

Release desires that cloud your inner view,
And in your heart, the light will breakthrough,
A beacon of love, pure and bright,
God's essence revealed, a guiding light.

The journey within is a path to grace,
Where love and faith converge in embrace,
In the silence of your soul's purest call,
God, the source of love, within you stands tall.

The Language of Heart

In the realm where divinity's presence does reside,
God's grace knows no bounds, far and wide,
Not the tongue's utterance, nor the mind's profound art,
But the language of the heart, the love, the very heart.

Words may falter, thoughts may stray,
But love's song in the heart, it finds its way,
For God, the listener of the pure and true,
In the language of love, our spirits renew.

The heart's whispers, sincere and profound,
Are the verses in which God's love is found,
Unspoken, unspoken, but eternally heard,
In the language of love, our souls are stirred.

So let your heart's language be love's sweet domain,
A symphony of devotion, free from any chain,
For God resides in the depths of the heart,
Listening to the language of love, far and wide.

Courage

In shadows deep, where fears reside,
A choice emerges from deep inside.
Fear is but a fleeting reaction,
Yet courage blooms as a steadfast fraction.

In trembling heart and anxious soul,
Fear's icy grip can take its toll.
But within us, a spark does burn,
A choice to make, a lesson to learn.

With every step into the unknown,
In courage, our strength has grown.
The decisions made, we stand tall,
Defying fear, we heed the call.

For courage is a flame that's lit,
From deep within, where doubts submit.
So let us decide, with hearts afire,
To face our fears and to climb higher.

The Key

In the garden of dreams, where goals reside,
Patience blossoms as a faithful guide.
A key that connects our efforts, so true,
To the gates of success, it leads us through.

In a world that rushes, in hurry and might,
Patience is a treasure and a soothing light.
It's not a delay, but a graceful art,
The steady rhythm of a hopeful heart.

With every step, with every trial,
Patience lends grace, it's not in denial.
It knows that success is a journey, so strong,
And every endeavor, each note of the song.

So let us nurture this virtue divine,
In the garden of patience, our dreams entwine.
For it's the key, the golden link,
Connecting our efforts, so success we'll drink.

The Choices

In the field of choices, where paths diverge,
Discipline is the bridge and our truest urge.
The cost it asks, it may seem high,
Yet it is but a greatness beneath the sky.

The price is steep in the land of regrets,
It seeks to keep a heavy lesson in life,
The 'could haves' and 'should haves,' they haunt the night,
But discipline shines as a lovely path.

With each early dawn, and every stride,
Discipline is there as our faithful guide.
It tempers desire and it shapes the soul,
To reach our goals and to make us whole.

So let's embrace the path of discipline,
For in its embrace, our dreams we'll chase.
The cost it may ask is a worthy bet,
Always less than the price of regret.

The Deeds

In the realm of action, where virtues shine,
Deeds speak volumes and they are the signs.
With hands that toil and hearts that care,
Deeds weave stories, beyond compare.

They paint a picture, bold and true,
Of who we are, of what we do.
In deeds, we find our noblest creed,
A testament to the life we love to lead.

For words can falter, promises can break,
But deeds, unwavering, their truth won't shake.
They build a legacy, they leave a trace,
Of the strength of character, in every case.

So let's be mindful in every way,
To let our deeds lead to light our day.
In this world where actions ring,
Deeds are the crown, they are the kings.

You Are the Real Journey

You are the real journey, a path untold,
In your heart's depths, a story to be unrolled.
With each step you take, a new world unfolds,
With a tale of courage and love, you became bold.

In every sunrise and sunset's gentle hue,
In laughter and tears and in every shade of blue,
You find the beauty, in the old and the new,
You are the real journey and your heart is true.

Embrace the challenges with a smile on your face,
 With kindness and grace, you'll leave a trace.
In your story, in your presence, in every place,
You are the real journey and a wondrous embrace.

So keep on walking, through life's unknown,
With love as your courage and you're never alone.
In your heart and soul, your spirit is shone,
You are the real journey, and you've beautifully grown.

Humility

Be humble, for even experts may err,
In the vast field of knowledge, we all learn more.
Mistakes are the stepping stones, where we learn and stir,
But in humility, wisdom and growth do concur.

With expertise gained through trials and struggles,
We may strive for perfection, yet we embrace life.
In the pursuit of greatness, amid joy and gloom,
Humility's beacon guides us through the bloom.

So be humble, my friend, and let your heart glow,
Even experts falter, it's a truth we know.
In the dance of life, let humility's river flow,
And happiness will flourish as a radiant, gentle glow.

Be Ready

Opportunity knocks as a visitor in disguise,
Creating appointments where dreams may arise.
But to seize the moment and to claim the prize,
You must be prepared, with open and eager eyes.

In the realm of possibilities, where fortunes reside,
Preparation is the key and a steadfast guide.
For success is not chance, but a journey we ride,
With hard work and readiness, we will win.

So polish your skills in the shadows of silence,
Be ready before the chance is fully grown.
Opportunity's embrace is a garden yet unknown,
You'll reap the rewards when your efforts are sown.

Embrace each moment with hope as your gear,
For opportunity and readiness are a powerful pair.
In the grand symphony of life, take your share,
Success is your destiny if you dare to care.

Everything and Nothing

In the depths of despair, you found your way,
Learned to give, not just to receive each day.
In hardship's embrace, you came to know,
The depths of hunger and the bitter woe.

You learned to give, not because of wealth,
But from the depths of your soul's truest self.
In the face of adversity, you found the grace,
To share your love and to brighten someone's space.

Your kindness is a beacon in the darkest night,
Inspiring others to join in the light,
Against poverty, despair, and fear,
With love, compassion, and sincere hope.

Your journey's testimony is a story of light,
A testament to the strength of human might.
You've shown the world what it means to be,
A giver of love, unconditionally free.

Focus on the Beauty

Amid the chaos, in the daily rush,
Pause for a moment and hush the worldly rush.
Think of the beauty that surrounds your way,
Let gratitude guide you through each day.

Embrace the smiles and laughter's grace,
In every kind heart and in every warm embrace.
For beauty's not just in the sights you see,
It's in the love, the moments, and memories.

So think of the beauty, both near and far,
And let it fill your heart like a shining star.
With gratitude as your faithful guide,
You'll find happiness in each stride.

The world may have troubles, its share of strife,
But focus on beauty as it's the key to life.
In every moment, let your heart be free,
With gratitude and love, life's always a sweet melody.

Stillness of the Mind

In the stillness of the mind, a glimpse of the divine,
A truth profound, a wisdom that's thine.
For when the mind finds peace, it's God we find,
A sacred moment and a presence so kind.

In mindful silence, we touch the heavens above,
A connection to the universe, a boundless love.
For in the quiet moments, we truly see,
The essence of existence, in pure clarity.

But when the mind awakens, it's humankind's call,
To navigate this world, to rise and stand tall.
We think, we feel, we create and explore,
In the infinite possibilities, we forever implore.

So seek the balance, the rhythm that's true,
In the stillness, in action, in all that you do.
For within the mind's dance, there's a path to be had,
From God to mankind, to mastery and back.

Don't Worry – Be Happy

Worry is a shadow in the mind's domain,
Stealing joy, faking needless pain,
Its grip on us is an illusion,
And in truth, it's all in vain.

For worry, like a thief at night,
Try to take our peace and to steal our light,
Yet in our hearts, we hold the might,
To cast it out and take our flight.

With truth and love, our souls unite,
No more lost in fake worry's endless night,
We choose to live in the radiant light,
An optimistic path, pure and bright.

So let us free our hearts from those worries,
And let the words of wisdom steer our hearts,
Towards a life that's ever-clear,
Full of love, joy, abundance, and purposes, my dear.

War and Peace

In times of turmoil, when war may near,
Let's turn our hearts to faith, not fear,
For in the darkest hour, we shall steer,
Towards a world of peace, crystal clear.

In this symphony of nations, let us strive,
To keep the flames of hope and love alive,
With gratitude, let our spirits revive,
As we pray to our God, in whom we believe.

Though the drums of war may loudly beat,
Our faith in God is a sturdy seat,
He guides us to a love so sweet,
A peaceful world where all hearts can meet.

With courage, optimism, and unity strong,
We'll build a future where we all belong,
For the third world war, we'll prove wrong,
 By choosing peace, where we all throng.

So let us keep our faith and our trust,
 In God's grace; in Him, we must,
Find strength, love, and peace robust,
And to banish war, in Him we trust.

Transformations

In the dance of life, we find our way,
Through transformations, night to day.
With every change, we learn to see,
The mystery of great love, how it sets us free.

From caterpillar to butterfly, we soar,
In the cocoon of change, we're reborn once more.
Embracing the unknown, we find our grace;
Transformations lead us to a brighter place.

We embark the energetic souls and lovely lessons,
Leaving our mark on this journey,
Our spirits take flight with hope and trust,
For in the mystery of change, we find our inner light.

So, let's celebrate each twist and turn,
Through transformations, we truly learn.
To love the mystery and to embrace the unknown,
With faith and love, our beliefs are grown.

Keep Smiling

For in the moment, we wished to soar,
Higher than all who'd come before.
Our hearts were filled with ambition's fire,
But in that path, we lost our true desire.

In the race to reach that lofty peak,
We found that happiness was what we'd seek.
For in the chase for fame and gold,
We'd forgotten the truths of life.

In the end, we've realized it's true:
To keep smiling, no matter what we go through.
Miraculous moments can still be found,
In the beauty of life, in each sight and sound.

So let us learn and let us grow,
With love and kindness, our hearts aglow.
In this journey, we'll find our way,
To a brighter, more beautiful, and truthful day.

The Unlimited One

In the truths of possibilities, we've just begun,
Don't limit the "Unlimited One."
Through His grace, miracles are in store,
Anything is possible, forever and more.

With faith as our guide, we'll boldly dare,
To reach heights unknown, to love and to care.
In His grace, we'll find our way,
Even on the darkest, stormiest day.

For the "Unlimited One" knows no end,
In His love, we turn kind.
No limits can hold back our dreams,
In His grace, life gleams and beams.

The Connections

In this world, so vast and wide,
Human connection is a precious tide.
A heartfelt bond, guiding afar,
It's the most beautiful truth by far.

In every smile, in every gaze,
In connections, our souls set ablaze.
Lovely threads that tie us together,
In these bonds, we find strength forever.

The faithful ties that we create,
In each other's lives, they resonate.
Guiding us through life's winding way,
In human connection, we'll always stay.

So let's cherish this gift, so divine,
For in connection, our spirits entwine.
In this world, it's the most important art,
A beautiful treasure close to the heart.

The Aim

In the realm of archery, a tale we find,
Where arrows take flight, with purpose in heart.
A good archer, you see, is known not by his quiver,
But by the aim in his heart and a purpose that is too strong.

For it's not in the arrows, but in the intent,
That the true skill of the archer is clearly meant.
His aim is his compass, his dreams set his course,
With every shot he takes, he shows no remorse.

In the face of the target, he stands firm and bold,
With patience and precision, his story unfolds.
In life, too, we can learn from this creed,
To aim for our dreams, with unwavering focus.

So remember, my friend, in your journey through life,
It's not in your failures, but in your inner strength.
A good archer is known not by his arrows,
But by the aim in his heart and a purpose so sincere.

Solitude

In solitude's embrace, our purpose comes alive,
A quiet space where dreams and hopes will thrive.
Amidst the stillness, truth and faith unite,
In solitude, the heart takes its rightful flight.

Loveliness in every thought and in every sigh,
A touching grace beneath the endless sky.
Faith blooms like flowers in the spring,
In solitude, we find our inner wings.

With energy untamed, our spirits rise high,
Realistic dreams we dare to explore.
In solitude, we craft our beautiful destiny,
A fantastic world where we're actually meant to be.

So beautiful is this journey we embrace,
In solitude's sweet, solitary space.
Amazingly, we find our purpose comes true,
In solitude, our lives begin anew.

Rising

In a world where shadows often fall,
We stand to heed a higher call.
To motivate, to empower, and to encourage all,
So they may rise when life's trials enthrall.

In the journey, we'll walk by their side,
Lifting them up with unwavering love.
For in unity, our strength will grow,
A realistic path where dreams can flow.

A heartfelt promise to support and care,
With amity and love, we'll be there.
This kind and faithful act we pledge,
Will create a better world from edge to edge.

With fabulously resilient souls combined,
We'll help each other with hearts entwined.
In this incredible quest, we shall engage,
To motivate, empower, and encourage, at every stage.

Solo and Strong

When you meet someone solo and strong,
In their uniqueness, there is a melody's song.
Lovely souls who stand on their own,
In solitude, their strength is brightly shone.

Touching lives with wisdom's embrace,
In their presence, we realize a special grace.
Fabulous and fearless, they walk their way,
With unwavering faith, day by day.

Truthful to themselves, they proudly stand,
Realistic dreams, they grasp with their heart.
Energetic sparks ignite their path,
In the realm of solitude, they find their strength.

For those solo and strong, a gift so rare,
Their faith and strength is a love to bear.
In the symphony of life, they have their role,
Recognize their worth, let your heart be whole.

The Right Thing

In a world of choices, clear and true,
A path to follow, I'll share with you.
"Do the right thing," the wisdom speaks,
For your heart and the world, the path it seeks.

In each decision, let kindness bloom,
In your actions, dispel the gloom.
For when you act with love and grace,
Miracles unfold in life's embrace.

The time will come, the stars align,
When deeds of goodness brightly shine.
For in the moments when your heart is pure,
Miracles and wonders will be the cure.

So, remember well the lesson dear,
To do what's right, without fear.
In this journey of life, make each day sing,
Miracles unfold when you do the right thing.

The Prayer

In a world where words can wound and scar,
Choose kindness over judgments, near and far.
Never put people down; let this be your creed,
For through compassion, our hearts truly feed.

Pray for them, instead of casting a stone,
Let your empathy and understanding be shown.
In the darkest of times, be a guiding light,
With prayers that can heal, with all your might.

Kindness in your heart, a gift so grand,
As you uplift others to the angel's heavenly land.
Realistic in your hopes, as you intercede,
For the broken, the lost, and those in need.

Supportive arms reach out and embrace,
A world that's torn, in need of grace.
For when you pray for others, my friend,
You'll find in their healing, your own beautiful soul.

A Beautiful Rhyme

Loving what you do is a treasure so rare,
And happiness blooms beyond compare.
Freedom's sweet song is a beautiful rhyme,
And in the dance of your passions, it's your precious time.

In each task and journey, a heart that's true,
Faithful to your purpose, in all that you pursue.
Realistic in your goals, and steadfast you'll be,
As you chase your dreams, both wild and free.

So, remember, my friend, this truth so clear,
In doing what you love, you find your way.
Freedom and happiness, hand in hand,
As you embrace the world, take a great stand.

The Fragile Moments

In the fragility of moments, life's reality weaves,
A light of beauty, where the heart believes.
Though delicate, they shine with an inner grace,
These moments are like fragile petals in life's embrace.

In their fleeting dance, we find the strength to thrive,
For even fragile, they teach us how to truly live.
In truth, they reveal the essence of our being,
Moments, fragile and pure, so freeing.

As realistic as the sunrise, as truthful as the dawn,
They inspire us to carry on when hope is there.
In their simplicity, we find the grandest of all,
The beauty in fragility, standing tall.

So let us be inspired by these moments, so fine,
For in their fragility, our lives brightly shine.
In their loveliness, we find the strength to cope,
Moments, still beautiful and the greatness of life's hope.

A Small Mistake

There's a truth we all must embrace,
That failing to attempt is a small mistake.
For in each honest effort, we find our greatest art,
A testament to the courage that resides within our heart.

In the face of challenges, don't let your spirit wane,
For even if you fall, you're stronger than the pain.
Embrace the imperfections, learn from every fall,
With determination and persistence, you'll conquer it all.

The path to greatness is paved with signs, it's true,
And those who dare to try emerge anew.
With faith in your abilities, you'll rise high,
For failing to attempt is a small failure in life.

So when a doubt attempt to hold you back,
Remember that you have the strength, sometimes you may not
realize.
And in each attempt, you'll find growth and resilience,
A journey filled with wisdom, beauty, and brilliance.

The Opinion

Amid the noise of voices, bold and loud,
Hold your ground, for your own path you seek.
In the realm of life, diverse and grand,
Don't let others' opinions take command.

Their words may swirl like a misjudging storm,
But in your heart, you must learn to trust.
For the energy that's uniquely you,
Radiates with a brilliance, ever true.

In the simplicity of being your authentic self,
You'll find the strength and gather inner wealth.
With every step you take, be energetic and free,
In the mirror of truth, your reflection you'll see.

The world's judgments and doubts, let them fade,
Your own worth and vision, do not evade.
In faith, stay faithful to your own song,
You are majestic, in your own way, strong.

Forget the Mistakes

In the journey of life, we may stumble and fall,
Mistakes, like shadows, on our path they may sprawl.
But in their midst, there is a lesson, strong and true,
Let's forget the errors, and then, the wisdom accrue.

Each become a teacher, though we may not see,
In the moment's chaos, or the heart's agony.
For within the errors, there's always a gem concealed,
A chance for growth and a new destiny revealed.

Majestic is the resilience that we find,
In learning from stumbles, leaving no regrets behind.
Inspirational are the stories that arise,
From those who've faced darkness but lifted their eyes.

Forget the mistakes, but remember the way,
They've shaped your character till this very day,
For within each misstep, there's a gift to be sought,
In this beautiful, touching, and lovely journey of life.

The Strength to Fly

Hope is a wish and a radiant beam,
Amidst the darkest, it's a gleam.
In shadows deep, it takes its flight,
A beautiful light through the endless night.

Inspirational, kind, and always true,
There is a force that helps us carry through.
Optimistic, faithful, and it is so bright,
Hope is the beacon in the darkest night.

Fabulous and fantastic is its embrace,
It shows us that there's a brighter place.
Truthful, as it keeps up our spirits so high,
In hope, we really find the strength to fly.

So, let hope's light forever shine,
In every heart, in every line.
For in its glow, we'll find our way,
Through darkness to a brighter day.

Believe in Yourself

In your heart, find the strength to dwell,
Believe in yourself; you're a mighty soul.
With optimism's light, you can excel,
With your faith and your spirit to explore more and more.

In the mirror of life, you're unique and bright,
A faithful journey, with each step so right.
With truth and belief, you'll reach your height,
Stay realistic and touching in your own light.

Amazing potential within you resides,
Fantastic dreams in your heart abides.
With love, faith, and determination as your guides,
Encouraging whispers in your soul, they reside.

So, remember always, in your heart's embrace,
The beauty of believing is strength and grace.
In simplicity, you'll find your place,
Always believe in yourself in life's lovely chase.

A Great Man

A man is great, not failure-free, it's true,
But the failure never could stop him.
In majesty, he rises through each fall,
As an inspirational spirit, he heeds the call.

Fantastic are the lessons we learn in each defeat,
Realistic struggles and faith, as his journey's heartbeat.
Energetic, he persists through every test,
With faithful hope, he gives his best.

In truth, he finds real strength in the stormy sea,
Mighty and lovely, his spirit really is.
Guiding others, he leads with grace,
Touching hearts with his resilient embrace.

So remember, greatness in the face of struggle,
Simple and clear is the story of life.
For a man is truly defined, it's true,
By how he rises and by the love he gives when trials accrue.

Sustained by Love

In life's grand scheme, we rise above,
With dreams sustained by love, faith, and hope.
Guiding lights that lead us on,
Inspirational and true, from dusk 'til dawn.

With every step, our hearts become bright,
A touch of miracle, a ray of light, a beautiful ray of love.
In this journey, we all must cope,
For every dream is sustained by love.

In the real world, where dreams are spun,
Mighty forces are not easily undone,
Keep it simple, let your spirit take flight,
For every dream in life is sustained by love.

The Pathway

In the depths of your heart, a dream takes flight,
Guided by God's hand, in the gentlest light.
Faithful and true, with love as your chart,
You'll find a pathway, a miraculous art.

Your heart became bright, like a radiant sun,
Mighty and phenomenal, your journey's begun.
Inspirational whispers, a divine, timeless cue,
A positive force, forever renewed.

A token of truth, refreshing and clear,
With love as your mission, you'll conquer all hearts,
For if you truly want, with a soul that's inspired,
God's pathway awaits; in you, it's pursued.

Once More

In each birth, a beautiful story unfolds,
As life's miracles, a wonderful tale retold.
Sincere and faithful, on this winding road,
Sensible dreams, in each life bestowed.

Lovely are the chances, each one anew,
Amazing adventures awaiting you here,
With cheerful flame, your spirit's aglow,
Vitalizing whispers, the way you'll go.

Productive steps on this wonderful quest,
In each exit's journey, you're truly blessed.
Incarnations reveal what's in store,
Gorgeous destinations you'll explore once more.

In Unity We Trust

When religions unite, in harmony we stand,
Divisive grip of politics released from our hands.
Wealth is no longer a measure of worth, as we see,
And race, just a shade in our humanity.

With love and compassion, our faith takes its place,
Realistic and truthful, our shared human grace.
Inspirational visions of unity's grand theme,
A fantastic, miraculous, heartwarming dream.

This touch of the divine is so genuinely real,
Brings us together as a positive ideal.
In the end, we find what truly defines us,
As one human family, in unity we trust.

Kindness

Life blooms when kindness takes its flight,
Embracing the wishes of the needy, facing the deepest night.
Heartfelt and true, in this courageous quest of life,
Truthful love emerges, at the kindness of many hearts.

Amazingly, they lead to "the light of insight,"
Inspirational radiance, shining so bright.
Positively guiding, like the northern star,
Gratitude's flame, from near to far.

Kind people help, without much questions,
They leave a trail, in each and every tests,
Leaving an impact, in every heart they touch,
Allowing it to spread through many more kind hearts.

Kindness within is a fantastic might,
Guiding your journey, both day and night.
With readiness to embrace each soul's plight,
And confidence shines forth as a beautiful beacon of light.

Let's Find Our Way

In a world of noise, let's find our way,
To listen without interruption, night and day.
With open hearts and ears so keen,
We'll build our bond like a beautiful dream.

Let's share without hesitation the joys we find,
The laughter, the tears, and the truth of our hearts,
In every moment, big or small,
Let's be one to share and care.

To speak without hatred, let kindness reign,
Let words be bridges, not causes of pain.
In understanding and love, we'll unite forever,
To make the world a bit brighter than ever.

In this journey, we'll be authentic and true,
Progressive souls with so much treasures to pursue.
With hearts that beat in a positive rhyme,
Together, we'll stand the test of time.

Bloom with Grace

Wherever life plants you, bloom with grace,
In every challenge, find your rightful place.
With courage and faith, you'll rise above,
In the garden of life, showered with love.

Let sanguinity be your guiding star,
Move ahead, no matter how near or far.
Embrace each moment of every new day's start,
In your beautiful bloom, reveal your heart.

With truth as your strength, stand tall and true,
For life's twists and turns, you'll gracefully move through.
Inspirational messages come from the soul of all to tell you,
That you're a fantastic blossom and a real testament to love.

Never Hate

Carry a heart that never hates,
In kindness and love, let your spirit enlight.
Carry a smile that never fades, shining bright,
Spreading joy and warmth from morning to night.

Carry a touch that never hurts, gentle and kind,
In your gentle embrace, many will find solace.
With faith in your soul, let these virtues rise high,
A beautiful path in life, with love as your great sigh.

The Big Purpose

When the purpose is big enough, we find the strength to rise,
To move the mountains, to reach the skies, with a fire in our
eyes.
With hearts ablaze and dreams so high, we stand so tall and
true,
In every step, we'll be strong, with a purpose to pursue.

Courageous souls, we journey on; the path may twist and turn,
But in our hearts, the purpose burns, a great lesson we will
learn.
In valleys deep and mountains steep, we'll climb with
steadfast stride,
For in our purpose, we confide, as life's great waves we ride.

Through challenges and darkened days, we'll hold the torch
of light,
With faith and truth as our guiding stars, we'll conquer every
sight,
No matter how the tempest roars or obstacles may appear,
With purpose driving us, my dear, we'll cast the love so dear.

For in this purpose, we unite, a force that can't be stilled,
A boundless well of strength and grace, with love and dreams
fulfilled.
So stand tall and faithful, with hearts full of grace,
With a purpose so big, we'll find our rightful place.

A Tasty Dish

Success is a tasty dish, a feast for those who dare,
With courage as your spice, the flavor fills the air.
Take a chance, reach out your hand, to taste the sweet delight,
In every daring effort, you'll find your own guiding light.

The journey may be winding, with hurdles in your way, but its fine,
But with each step you conquer, your dreams will lead the way.
So dare to chase your passion, with faith in every try,
For success is a tasty dish, a lovely treat beneath the sky.

Determination

A desire sparks a yearning deep within your soul,
But a mere wish alone won't make your dreams whole.
A decision takes you closer to the path you long to tread,
Yet it's determination that ignites the fire, it's said.

With resolute heart, you face the trials that may appear,
And every obstacle you conquer makes your purpose crystal clear.
So let determination be your guide, your unwavering guide,
It changes everything, and in its light, you'll ride.

With steadfast will, you mold your destiny anew,
The world transforms around you, your dreams begin to bloom.
A force that's undying, it empowers every stride,
Determination changes everything, as you rise high with joy, love, and faith.

Everyone Is Gifted

In a world where dreams are sown and sown,
Lies a truth that's often left unknown.
"Everyone is gifted," so they say,
But some, their talents hide away.

With hearts that beat and souls so vast,
We're all unique, from first to last.
In each of us, a gift does dwell,
A tale of miracle, only time will tell.

Unwrap your package, let it shine,
For in your gift, your path you'll find.
Though hidden, deep within your core,
A treasure waiting to explore.

Embrace the truth, let doubts be cleared,
For every soul is wondrous, revered.
Be faithful to your inner light,
And watch it guide you through the night.

People, Places and Memories

As we start to walk on the path, we find our way,
Through places seen, where memories play.
The best things we cherish, a truth so serene,
Are the places we've roamed, the people we've been with.

In distant horizons, under the sun's gleam,
We've wandered and explored, like in a dream.
From mountaintops high to the ocean's serene,
Each place leaves a mark, a memory, a scene.

And as we walk on this life's winding lane,
The memories we gather, both joy and pain,
Are etched in our souls; they forever remain,
A testament to journeys, our heart's sweet refrain.

So here's to the places, the people, the past,
The memories we've made, they forever will last.
In the book of our life, these moments convene,
The best things in life, the tapestry we've seen.

Money: Test of Humanity

In the realm of human quest and strife,
Money stands as a marker of our life,
A discovery, profound and true,
Revealing human nature, through and through.

Yet, amidst the greed and worldly sway,
There's a Godly path, a different way,
To use this currency, this earthly treasure,
For kindness, love, and shared goodwill, without measure.

In God's grace, we find a guiding light,
To use money well and to do what's right,
To help the needy and to lift those in despair,
Money as a blessing, for love and care.

For in this world, money has blessed space,
A reflection of our true human race,
Let it also define our inner soul,
And, let Godly wisdom be our ultimate goal.

Two Words

In life, two words hold immense weight:
Yes and no, decisions we contemplate,
In moments missed, the stories untold,
For saying them wrong, our fate can be changed.

Yes, the word of opportunity and chance,
Yet, delayed, still it can make life's music dance,
The harmony of moments and melodies we'll miss,
By hesitating to say yes soon, in moments of bliss.

No, a shield to protect our precious time,
But said too fast, can be a costly crime.
Sometimes a boundary, a choice we must make,
Yet, too swift a no, can cause hearts to ache.

In the realm of these two, we must find the key,
To say yes with wisdom, and no, with empathy,
For in balance, they create life's divine flow,
These two words, in their essence, a sacred tableau.

In the reality of existence, where we weave and grow,
The power of yes and no, a divine art to show,
In every choice, a chance to learn and grow,
With God's guidance, our inner compass to follow.

Your Divine Revelation

In the realm of dreams and aspirations, we tread,
Passion, the fire in our hearts, widespread,
But until it meets determination's resolute might,
The full extent of our strength stays out of our sight.

God's guidance lights the path we trace,
As passion ignites our hearts with grace,
Determination fuels the fire so bright,
Turning visions into tangible, wondrous light.

In the crucible of time, our mettle's truly known,
As sweat and tears water seeds we've sown,
For the union of passion, determination, and vision,
Is a divine recipe, a life-altering decision.

So, seek God's wisdom, let it be your guide,
As you journey on life's magnificent ride,
In the fusion of passion, vision, and dedication,
Lies your true potential, your divine revelation.

The Secret of Trials

On our pathway of life, we often find,
For every trial, a miracle designed.
When darkness veils the path we tread,
A miracle unveils, like words unsaid.

In challenges we face, we may despair,
But hidden miracles, we're often unaware.
With faith as our guide and hope held tight,
Miracles emerge from the depths of night.

In tears that fall and hearts that ache,
Miracles blossom, without a mistake.
For in our struggles, we find the grace,
Of miracles that light our life's embrace.

So, let not despair weigh down your soul,
Miracles, like whispers, make us whole.
With faith, love, and purpose in our sight,
God's miracles shine in the darkest night.

The Priceless Things

In the test of the time, a truth does shine,
The priceless treasures, the memories divine.
With the right people by our side,
Majestic moments in our hearts reside.

The laughter shared and tears we've shed,
In those cherished moments, the soul is fed.
Through trials and triumphs, hand in hand,
True friendships by God's gracious plan.

The golden hours with kindred souls,
In their presence, life's purpose unfolds.
Through every season, joy or strife,
The faithful bonds, the threads of life.

For worldly riches may come and go,
But these memories, like an eternal flow.
In the tapestry of time, they gleam and glow,
 God's gift to us, in His love, we know.

So, hold dear the moments with the right ones,
For in those memories, love takes flight.
A Godly truth that we must embrace,
The most priceless things in life, all by His grace.

Willpower

In the face of defeat, a chance to renew,
Failure, the stepping stone, to begin anew.
Willpower, a force that conquers all might,
Guiding us through darkness, into the light.

With each stumble, wisdom's seeds are sown,
Opportunity blooms where courage is shown.
A canvas refreshed, a chance to redraw,
Failures pave the way to find our true awe.

Godly strength within, a divine spark ignites,
Enthusiasm soaring to incredible heights.
Energetic spirits, in trials, find their place,
Heartfelt resolve, an unwavering grace.

So embrace failures, they're but a mere bend,
For starting afresh is where victories ascend.
Each setback a lesson, a chance to refine,
Failure's the path where true greatness will shine.

The Design of Life

Within the tapestry of existence, wisdom's essence weaves,
Faith, the silent whisper that the soul believes.
A bridge to the divine, a lantern in the night,
Guiding hearts through shadows with unwavering light.

Hope, a delicate petal in life's resilient bloom,
A melody of dreams, dispelling sorrow's gloom.
In the garden of possibilities, where aspirations soar,
Hope paints the canvas of tomorrow evermore.

Patience, a river that serenely winds its way,
Navigating trials with grace, come what may.
Time's gentle sculptor, molding strength within,
In the dance of patience, victories begin.

Love, the universal language, a boundless sea,
Where hearts find solace in sweet unity.
Summed up in these threads, a wisdom divine,
Faith, hope, patience, love—a divine design of life.

Something about the Nothing

In the canvas of azure, the blue sky unfurls,
Whispers of a tale, as the sizzling wind whirls.
The dancing ocean, a liquid ballet,
Each wave, a chapter in the story they convey.

Beneath twinkling stars, secrets softly told,
The shining sun, a ballad of warmth and gold.
Mind-blowing moon, with mysteries to share,
Weaves its verses in the night's tender air.

Among sand dunes, where time's footprints erase,
Twisting storms echo the tumultuous embrace.
Flowing river, a narrative gently revealed,
Shaping rocks in silence, stories concealed.

Drizzling rain, a poetic cascade from above,
Moving clouds narrate a dance of endless love.
In this symphony, all elements play a part,
A tale of being something from nothing, etched in every heart.

A Sprinkle of Joy

In the dance of life, pessimists bemoan the waves,
Their complaints echo, lost in the vast ocean's caves.
Optimists, buoyant, anticipate joy's embrace,
Riding the waves, finding solace in each trace.

Yet, the realist, wise navigator of the wind's sway,
Views the unseen currents, charts a deliberate way.
Adjusting the sails, steering through uncertainty's gale,
They find purpose in the journey, a steadfast tale.

"Leave a little sparkle," whispers the guiding light,
In every corner you dwell, in the shadows of the night.
Wherever you tread, let courage pave the road,
For a sprinkle of joy is the greatest story ever told.

The Insight

In the canvas of perception, a masterpiece unfurls,
Vision, an art, sees the hidden, the invisible pearls.
Brushing strokes of insight on the palette of the mind,
It unveils secrets, treasures that others may not find.

Through the lens of dreams, where possibilities reside,
The unseen becomes vivid, in imagination's stride.
Eyes that perceive beyond the tangible, the known,
Witness the miracles where inspiration has grown.

A symphony of clarity, in the realm of the unseen,
Vision is the poet's verse, the artist's serene sheen.
With every gaze, a revelation, a glimpse of the divine,
In the art of insight, the invisible does shine.

Three Best Gifts

Among the three best gifts, you can give and still keep,
Are your word, your smile and a grateful heart.
A smile is a currency that transcends every part,
And in the treasury of words, kindness is a timeless art.

A grateful heart is a compass, guiding life's chart,
Holding onto blessings, it is a treasure to impart.
This truth is a beacon, though to some it may seem apart,
Shines bright, dispelling illusion's fleeting dart.

Align your focus, thoughts, and let these solutions do the art,
For in challenges faced, they are the wisdom to impart.
Do good for others, a ripple and a benevolent spark,
In the cosmic dance, for sure, goodness returns as a cosmic arc.

Truly Blessed

Beneath the canvas of forgiving grace,
A heart unfolds its tender embrace,
Softening the edges of the darkest past,
Weaving threads of resilience, steadfast.

Eyes, like dawn's gentle light, seek the best,
Painting hues of love in life's vast quest.
In every soul lies a shimmering spark,
As kindness and empathy leave their mark.

The beauty in others is a mindful sanctuary,
Where negativity loses its relentless reign.
Joy and serenity find their peace,
As the life adorned is truly blessed.

A Home

Open wide the door of your heart,
For those who are willing to stay forever.
The lovely hearts, companions of the soul,
Together, woven, a tapestry whole.

Wondrous whispers of connection, like gentle air,
In this heart's haven, they find a lair.
Stay, dear ones, in the warmth and glow,
A haven where love continues to grow.

A room where time can't wear away,
Welcoming hearts that choose to stay.
In the dance of moments, in love of the memories,
Heart is a home for those who claim your heart.

With Love

In the garden of your life, may joy bloom,
Let your tears transform to petals, colors in full plume.
May your years ahead be a tapestry so fine,
Woven with threads of love, a radiant design.

As you journey, may your vision be graced,
Colors of the world, in every hue embraced.
Let your insight be a mirror reflecting grace,
A reflection of beauty in every life's trace.

May meanings blossom in each passing day,
As moments unfolding in a memory ballet.
Let kindness emanate in the core of your heart,
A gentle melody, a soulful counterpart.

Let manifestations of gratitude, like petals, unfurl,
Life's symphony, a dance with joy in every swirl.
In the quietude, may peace find its abode,
A tranquil river where your soul's journey is stowed.

Climb to heights, yet rooted in humility,
A balance of grace in life's vast symphony.
May your smile become a beacon, radiant and true,
Illuminating the path, guiding others through.

In the tapestry of your own realities spun,
May God's guidance be your eternal sun.
Shine, oh special one, in beauty so rare,
You are cherished, beloved, beyond compare.

With LOVE…
Dr. HANEESH KHANI